To

_____

From

_____

Date

_____

When Someone You Love No Longer Remembers

WRITTEN BY
Cecil Murphey

ILLUSTRATIONS BY
Michal Sparks

HARVEST HOUSE PUBLISHERS

EUGENE, OREGON

When Someone You Love No Longer Remembers

Text Copyright © 2011 by Cecil Murphey
Art Copyright © 2011 by Michal Sparks

Published by Harvest House Publishers
Eugene, Oregon 97402
www.harvesthousepublishers.com

ISBN 978-0-7369-3871-6

Mr. Gifford B. Bowne II
Indigo Gates
1 Pegasus Drive
Colts Neck, NJ 07722
(732) 577-9333

Design and production by Garborg Design Works, Savage, Minnesota

Unless otherwise indicated, all Scripture verses are from the *Holy Bible*, New Living Translation, copyright ©1996, 2004. Used by permission of Tyndale House Publishers, Inc., Wheaton, IL 60189 USA. All rights reserved.
Verses marked KJV are taken from the King James Version of the Bible.

Printed in China

11 12 13 14 15 16 17 18 19 / FC / 10 9 8 7 6 5 4 3 2 1

Contents

She No Longer Remembers

Barry didn't want to believe his wife had dementia. "She's a little forgetful," he said before he changed the subject.

It's more than being a little forgetful. For a long time Barry had to say those words to himself because he couldn't say them aloud.

Despite what his head knew, his heart fought the information. That's another way to express denial. To admit that her condition was more than forgetfulness also forced him to admit there would be no improvement. *She will remember less next week than she does today.*

For a long time Barry tried to cover for her, but eventually her condition became obvious. More and more often, friends asked questions about her behavior or her odd word choices.

"She no longer remembers," he finally said to a friend.

The confused look made Barry realize that he had to explain, but he could force out only three words: "She...can't...remember..."

His voice cracked and the friend spoke the forbidden word: "Alzheimer's?"

Barry nodded because his emotions hadn't allowed him to pronounce it.

The friend embraced him. "I'm sorry for her... I also know this will be a heavy burden on your shoulders."

Barry smiled then—perhaps for the first time in three months. *My friend understands.*

That was the beginning of being open and facing the reality. True, she no longer remembers, but it's more than that. She has dementia, but she has Barry beside her to walk down the road of no longer remembering.

Most of all, God walks with both of them through the deep, dark valley.

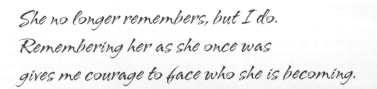

She no longer remembers, but I do. Remembering her as she once was gives me courage to face who she is becoming.

2

"He Will Only Get Worse"

"The first time I heard the doctor say those words, I cried," Ellen said. Then she wiped away her tears and begged the doctor, "Can't you give me any hope?"

Ellen wanted the doctor to say that he could slow the progression of her father's dementia or that there was an experimental drug that he wanted to try. Instead, the doctor shook his head. "I can offer you no hope that we can stop the disease."

Ellen cried again. As painful as those words were for her to absorb, they also enabled her to look ahead.

"It may sound strange to find hope and peace at such a time, but I did," she told me. "I knew the worst: my father will continue to deteriorate. Each day I will lose a tiny piece of him. But I also know I can call on God for daily strength to endure."

That's how Ellen coped for the next four years. "As I lost another part of him—which is the only way I knew how to say it—I held on to God's promise to be with me."

Dear loving God, I know he'll get progressively worse. Some days I try to deny it; other days I wonder how much longer before I lose him in the darkness from which there is no return. You promised, "The eternal God is your refuge, and his everlasting arms are under you" (Deuteronomy 33:27).

Hold me tightly, Lord, I need your comforting care right now.

9

The Rules Have Changed

JASON'S STORY

"Once you face the reality that your loved one suffers from dementia, your life changes," my friend told me, "and so does the loved one." As I absorbed those words, he said, "She may have been your mother, but now she becomes dependent on you as if you are her parent."

Before the onset of disease, the rules were different. She handled the checkbook and finances, but I've now become the bookkeeper, the business head, and person in charge.

It's not easy. Not only have the rules of life changed, but they did it without asking for my cooperation.

While I care for my mother, I also have to watch for the slightest change. Even though I know she won't improve, I still hope she'll recall something today that she couldn't remember a week ago.

When the rules changed, I received a double load. Not only did I take on the responsibility for caring, but I also had to take on the responsibility for serious self-caring—and I may tend to neglect the second. As I continue, some days the best I can do may be to remind myself to rely on God's promise: "I will never fail you. I will never abandon you" (Hebrews 13:5b).

The rules change and so does life.
God stays the same and enables me
to feel his love and compassion.

4

What's the Purpose in This?

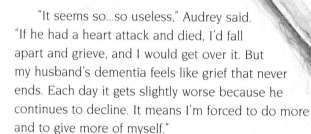

"It seems so...so useless," Audrey said. "If he had a heart attack and died, I'd fall apart and grieve, and I would get over it. But my husband's dementia feels like grief that never ends. Each day it gets slightly worse because he continues to decline. It means I'm forced to do more and to give more of myself."

Although Audrey isn't the first person to think that way (and won't be the last), she has to make choices each day. She can allow her thoughts to remain dark and focused on despair and meaninglessness, or she can change her perspective.

What if Audrey believed that she is exactly where she is now because of God's loving will for her? What if God called her to serve her loved one? What if it's God's will for her to be a faithful caregiver?

Jesus told a parable about the end of the age in which everyone would appear before him. "Then [Jesus] will say to those on his right, 'Come, you who are blessed by my Father, inherit the Kingdom prepared for you from the creation of the world...I was sick, and you cared for me...I tell you the truth, when you did it to one of the least of these my brothers and sisters, you were doing it to me!'" (Matthew 25:34b, 36b, 40).

What if God has called Audrey and me and many others to be among the blessed? What if we think of our caregiving for our loved one as divine service?

Each day I can remind myself:
When I do a loving thing for her,
I am doing something loving for Jesus.

"How Long Will I Hurt?"

TAMARA'S STORY

I wanted the agony and grief to end. But it won't—at least not for a long time. Alzheimer's disease (AD), or any form of dementia, isn't a disease with a known timeline. Some individuals survive a decade and many less than half that. No one knows when the end will come.

I forced myself to accept that I'll feel pain—loss and sadness—as long as my husband is alive. After he's gone, they tell me a different kind of grief takes over. Regardless of the type, it all hurts.

No matter how strong I am—and some days I feel extremely weak—Jesus Christ is with me, even in the darkest, loneliest moments. Occasionally I doubt, but most of the time I *know*, and I can say, "You are with me."

At moments I cry out, "Why can't it be over?" I think I've learned to cope only to discover new losses in my loved one.

"I felt as if she slipped away from me an inch at a time," one man said of his mother. "I tried to pull her back or to slow her down. Nothing helped, and that made my sadness grow."

A member of my support group said, "It helped me to remember that the deterioration wasn't her fault; it was simply the progression of the disease."

How long will I hurt?

No one can tell me, and that's not really my question, is it?

The question is probably closer to this: "God, will you lift this burden from me? How long will I have to suffer?"

And no one can give me the answer.

O Lord,
you have examined my heart
and know everything about me...
You go before me and follow me.
You place your hand of blessing
on my head...
How precious are your thoughts
about me, O God.

They cannot be numbered! (Psalm 139:1,5,17).

6

She Doesn't Deserve This

I've heard people wail that good people don't deserve the problems or heartbreak that come to them. They said that about those with AD and other serious illnesses or catastrophes. Taken as it is, the question says that people get only what they earn or deserve from the way they behave.

But it's not a matter of deserving or not deserving. Life doesn't function that way. Jesus says our heavenly Father "gives his sunlight to both the evil and the good, and he sends rain on the just and the unjust alike" (Matthew 5:45b).

And yet the statement is a natural reaction, especially when a loved one has a progressive illness. "It seems unfair," friends say. "Unjust. Not right."

No matter how I or anyone looks at the onset of AD, no one can explain the reason our loved one suffers.

That's one of life's unanswerable questions, but we can assure ourselves that God hasn't deserted us or our loved one.

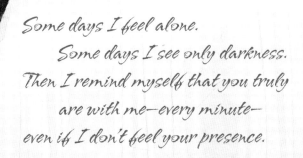

Some days I feel alone.
Some days I see only darkness.
Then I remind myself that you truly
are with me—every minute—
even if I don't feel your presence.

7

What He Feels

ELIZABETH'S STORY

In the days before we realized what was wrong, my father mixed up words. Once he referred to the car engine as an eggbeater. I knew what he meant from the context and I laughed. He didn't understand why I laughed.

After that, it became worse. He talked less. Sometimes I watched his face to read the clues about what he meant or wanted.

One evening, he rambled for two or three minutes, and his words seemed disjointed and nonsensical. The longer he talked, the more agitated he became. I opened my mouth to yell, "How can I help? I don't have any idea what you mean."

Just before I did that, I "heard" his confusion and sensed the pain on his face, mostly in his eyes. He knew something was wrong, and the more he tried to make himself understood, the more irritated he became.

I rubbed my hands across his cheek. He calmed down. Although I

never figured out what he tried to say, I learned an important lesson that evening: *What he feels is more important than what he can say.*

Because I love him, I reach out to comfort him and he needs that more than he needs me to understand what his words fail to express.

8

Reading Her Mind

PAUL'S STORY

Some days it feels as if I have to read my wife's mind. She can no longer express what she wants or means. But after 45 years of marriage, I've come to know her fairly well. At least I know her habits and her likes.

Sometimes it's simple. She wants one envelope of Equal and half a teaspoon of Coffee-mate, but I have to put in the sweetener first. On other occasions, I fight frustration trying to figure out what she wants. Sometimes I have to give up, but I'm getting better at figuring out meanings.

She can't understand what's on TV, and I doubt that she can read, but she retains many of her habits. When I turn on the evening news, she sits with her book open and occasionally glances at the screen—the way she used to do. As long as I can re-create our normal lifestyle, she's usually all right.

I tried to explain to a friend that I had become a mind reader. Although I don't think he meant to be cruel, he said, "How can you read a mind that's no longer there?"

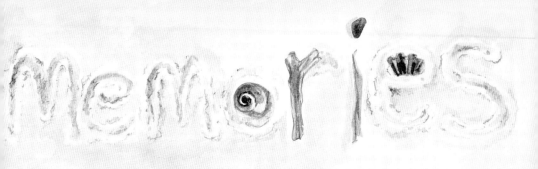

memories

"I read the memory," I said.

Later I thought about my answer, and it gave me great comfort. My wife and I won't make new memories together as we once did. Now I call on the past. Sometimes when she's agitated, I tell her about how nervous I was at our wedding or at the birth of our first child. Or I'll get out pictures of our Caribbean cruise. How much of the past she remembers, I don't know, but those simple things soothe her. I watch as the tension in her face relaxes. Sometimes I hold her hand, and she rewards me with a smile.

I can't read her mind, but I can read parts of her memory. That helps me know that she is still with me.

9

His Lost World

DORIS' STORY

I didn't know how to answer when my husband asked, "When's Robbie coming home?" Our oldest son, Robbie, died in Vietnam. The first time he asked that question, I foolishly said, "Robbie is dead." He became agitated and paced the room for almost an hour.

The next time he asked about Robbie (and at other times it would be a childhood friend or his mother), I would say something quiet such as, "I still miss Robbie."

Just a simple remark like that seemed to be enough. I learned it because I tried to put myself into his world. I envisioned him in a world of confusion where he grasped at tiny threads of memories. Simple, quiet answers are enough for him to know that I've entered into his lost world. And it is lost to him, but I'm with him. I also pray that he'll realize that God is with him through every dark, confused moment.

He doesn't need me to add to his lostness,
but he does need me to join him as he journeys
down a confused, unknown path.

10

Tricks of the Positive

WILMA'S STORY

It may seem devious, but it works. I try to read light, humorous books and rent comedies on DVD. And I laugh. It may be a little forced at times, but I laugh and applaud the simplest situations.

And it works. My husband smiles and sometimes he laughs. I don't think he has any idea what's going on, but he responds to the positive stimulus.

Here's another trick I learned: I sing his favorite songs—softly. I don't have much of a singing voice, but he doesn't notice. He has three favorite hymns: "No,

Not One," "What a Friend We Have in Jesus," and "In the Garden." Each of them go back to his days in Sunday school when his favorite teacher taught him to sing them before he could read the words. Occasionally he joins me in singing part of a stanza.

Sometimes I make sandwiches of peanut butter and grape jam, the kind of lunch he took all through high school. I love to watch him enjoy the treat. He carefully eats the crust first, all around the sandwich. (He once said that was the part he didn't like so he ate it first to get rid of it.)

I keep trying new tricks and improving on the old ones. And I discovered a wonderful secret: When he laughs, smiles, or remains calm, I feel better. The more positive I make the situation for him, the better and more optimistic I am.

Maybe one reason these things work is that
I did them for him.
And in doing something positive for him,
I help myself.

The Power of a Hug

HARRY'S STORY

Whenever anyone hugs Marilyn, her disposition improves. I don't know why it works, but it does. Perhaps it's the simple act of skin touching skin. Perhaps it's a reminder of childhood when most of us received an abundance of touches, hugs, and pats.

I wasn't much of a hugger, but I am now. I wrap my arms around her more than I ever did. She's now at the place where she doesn't hug back, but that's all right. Last week she let me hug her before she asked, "Who are you?"

"Someone who loves you," I said.

She smiled.

Whenever visitors come to our home, I ask them to embrace Marilyn. She doesn't fight it even though she rarely responds.

Any kind of skin touch helps. Sometimes when she's agitated, I take her hand and rub it gently. Or I rub lotion into her hands. A few times I've given her a foot massage.

I don't understand everything about touch,
but the more she moves away from me,
the more I rely on physical touch to connect with her.

12

Doing What He Can Do

I've always been an efficient person and don't like wasting time. One of the most difficult lessons I had to learn as a caregiver was to think of time differently. There is nothing to save and nothing to waste.

For now I am my husband's caregiver. That's a limiting definition, but it's the strongest and most accurate. On our wedding day I pledged myself to him, "for better or for worse."

I didn't expect him to be diagnosed with dementia; I didn't expect anything terrible to happen to either of us. But he has Alzheimer's, and he is the center of my world. My role is to help him enjoy what little he can right now.

One task that gives him pleasure is when I let him help me prepare a meal. I give him only the simplest tasks, and sometimes I have to show him how to do each thing.

Recently we made chocolate-chip cookies. He had more pleasure eating dough than doing anything else. He'd sneak dough inside his mouth and smile at me. I smiled back. I fed him a few bites with a spoon, and he liked that even better.

That was the good time, but there have also been cooking disasters. After I scrambled the eggs and before I could get them to the stove, he grabbed the dish and dumped everything into the garbage. We ate cereal that morning.

I want to keep him as independent as possible for as long as I can. He's quieter and more manageable when he's helping me.

I have to watch him carefully. It's not the level of intimacy I would like, but it's the level of intimacy we have. And I'm content.

I let him do what he can while he can.

13

Touching, Touching

"It was like learning a new language," he said. "By nature, I'm not a touchy-feely person, I'm the verbal type." He said he could easily talk about his wife's feelings or attitudes. "But she doesn't understand most of what I say."

He told me he struggled to change because he didn't like to be touched by others. He had come from a reserved family where they rarely demonstrated affection. His father used to say that embracing someone was too intimate to be done where others could watch.

"One day she began to cry, and I couldn't figure out what bothered her." He said that even after she stopped crying, she fidgeted, couldn't sit still, paced the room, and kept pointing at the windows.

Finally he got up, stood in front of her, and held her.

"The most amazing thing happened," he said. "Her body relaxed. She stared at me and smiled."

He led her to the sofa, helped her sit, and they held hands while they watched a movie on TV. She remained quiet for the next two hours.

"For a time, touching her hands or embracing her was my last resort." He smiled before he said, "But now I've learned the language of touch. It also reminds me how much I love her.

"Does she understand what I'm doing?" He scratched his chin a few times before he said, "I don't know how aware she is. But I do know she's calmer, and so am I."

I've learned the power of the first resort: I touch her.

14

Silent Moments

WENDELL'S STORY

My wife had always liked noise. We taught our children to sleep through the night by playing recorded music in the next room. Friends often visited while the children were growing up. Sometimes we had two television sets going. At least once a month, we held dinner parties with six to eight people.

That's changed now. The house remains quiet. It's taken me a long time to get used to the silence. We stopped inviting friends to our house because the presence of other people confused her. We stopped going to restaurants unless we got there before the evening crowd.

As I learned, a lot of noise—whether voices or music—upsets and confuses her.

Sometimes she becomes angry and yells. At other times she makes quick movements that show her agitation. It seems as if she frantically searches for the source of the noise. Even if two conversations are going

on, she doesn't know which one she's supposed to listen to and probably understands neither.

It's been a big adjustment for me. For a long time I called them the silent moments—times when the least noise troubled her. Now I call them quiet moments. I read more; I sometimes sit and pray quietly.

Her disease has caused me to go inward and to depend on God's strength. The quiet time has become peaceful and relaxed.

I don't do well with silent moments; but I've learned to embrace the quiet ones.

15

Laughing a Lot

KENNETH'S STORY

She laughs when I do, but the vacant look in my wife's eyes tells me she doesn't understand the humor. It's all right though. I don't question her or try to explain.

Because I don't know what goes on inside her, I can't judge her reactions. But I've noticed one thing—she likes humor, and afterward she's calmer.

Is her laughter purely copying my behavior? Does she grasp anything? I worried over that for days. Finally, I decided that it doesn't matter. She's engaged in laughing. And she's more manageable, especially when I sense she's going to become stubborn.

I subscribe to free jokes on the Internet. My friends forward cartoons and funny sayings. Sometimes I read them aloud. I hold up the printed pictures, point to them, and laugh. She usually laughs as well.

In a way it's strange. I keep trying to find ways to make her laugh so

she feels better. I think it works for her. It also works for me.

When she gets on my nerves—and that happens a lot—I distract myself by laughing at a joke. Sometimes I call my best friends, Bob or Mickey. I call them because both have that amazing ability to lift my spirits just by the way they talk to me.

So now I know that humor works for her. And for me. That makes it worth doing.

It's not always easy to laugh, but I'm learning.

35

16

His Name Is Homer

ELLEN'S STORY

Our six-year-old granddaughter brought a stuffed penguin with her one day when she visited. Her grandfather reached out for it, and she handed it to him. He held the bird and stroked it.

"His name is Homer," our granddaughter said. After a few minutes she reached for Homer, but he held it tightly and wouldn't give it back. Before she started to cry, her mother said, "Honey, give Homer to your grandfather. He gets lonely."

"I'll buy you a new penguin," I said.

"Okay," she said. She studied her grandfather for a while and showed him how to stroke the bird. "Homer likes it when you do it this way." She moved his hands slowly down from the top of the penguin's head.

He smiled, and she talked to him and told him that Homer came from Antarctica and gets lonely. "So you have to hold him tight so he won't cry for his mama."

She turned back to her parents and to me. "You're right. Grandpa needs Homer. At the store you can buy me his brother."

That afternoon I watched my husband, and he held Homer tightly. I made no attempt to take Homer away from him. When it came time for his bath, I said, "Homer likes to watch." I placed the toy just beyond his reach. "When you're done, you can hold him again."

Some days my husband will spend a long time with Homer; other days, he hardly seems to notice. I keep the toy in the same place. The other day he picked up the bird and smiled. "Homer," he said and petted his toy.

I've also placed an afghan and two soft pillows nearby. When he gets stressed, he sits and strokes them. Sometimes he smiles at me.

God, enable me to rejoice in the little things that make him happy. Show me how to embrace quiet times when he's content. Most of all, remind me that you're with him and with me. When I remember that, I'm happy and content.

Please Look at Me

"When I take my wife to church," Chuck said, "I become invisible."

He said people stare at her, a few try to talk to her, but most of them hurry by so they don't have to speak. "One woman pronounced each word as if Phyllis were hard of hearing and it might help her understand, and of course it didn't."

Marlene was glad the people in her church knew about her husband, but added, "I wish they'd see me." She said she'd hear a few perfunctory questions about how she was doing, but the real questions were about him.

"You know what hurts me the most? They don't look at me. They talk to me and they talk about my husband, but they won't make eye contact. It's as if I don't exist. I've wanted to shout to the members of our Sunday school class, 'Look at me! I'm here. I'm alive and I understand your words!'"

Marlene was able to acknowledge the members' difficulties in knowing what to say or how to behave, but she still wished they would look at her.

Your gaze is always on me.
You're not embarrassed or ashamed.
Because of you, Lord, I can look at others
    even if they can't look closely at me.

What Happened to My Dreams?

You probably had dreams, some of which you could have fulfilled had you worked steadily at them. But you couldn't follow those yearnings, and you ended up quite differently from where you thought you'd be.

If you're called to care for someone with dementia, your dreams are put aside, ignored, or forgotten. Without applying for the position, you fell into the job description of caregiver.

In your worst moments, you probably think or say words such as these:

- "I have no life of my own."
- "I can't do any long-term planning."
- "Some days I feel like an unpaid servant."

It's all right to feel that way.

Regret is natural, and sometimes you need to think about yourself and your desires. You need to find ways to enjoy moments even if you can't fully embrace the days or the months.

It becomes easier if you remind yourself that this is your role *right now.* Even though it didn't fit into your life plan, this is where God has placed you. Instead of fretting over the dreams you can't fulfill, perhaps you can learn to say, "This is God's will for me. I can draw on his strength."

You can remind yourself of the promises:
"When they call on me, I will answer;
I will be with them in trouble.
I will rescue and honor them" (Psalm 91:15).

I didn't ask for this assignment.
But as I serve my loved one,
I'm also serving my loving God.

19

All My Fears

Of course you worry or you're fearful. It's a natural reaction, so don't think of yourself as being weak or sinful. You're the caregiver, and you love someone who remembers less and less.

In those quiet moments when you're alone, anxieties and worries attack. It may be when you try to sleep or when you're having your morning coffee. The questions pound inside your head and heart.

- "What's going to happen to me?"
- "Who'll take care of me if I get sick?"
- "How can I keep on with this?"
- "My nerves are on edge, and I feel I'm going to snap."

As dreadful as it may seem, those fears and worries are issues you need to face. Some of them may be irrational; others are real and frightening. You can do relaxation exercises, read inspirational thoughts,

repeat favorite poems, or sing uplifting songs to yourself. Discover what works for you.

One of the caregivers of someone with Alzheimer's said that she copied several verses from the Bible and kept them next to her bed. She read them repeatedly. "I wasn't good at memorizing, but there was one I quoted slowly several times: 'Thou wilt keep him in perfect peace, whose mind is stayed on thee: because he trusteth in thee'" (Isaiah 26:3, KJV).

*Lord, remind me that you're with me now
and you'll be with me through every day and every ordeal.
Quiet the storms of my heart and give me your perfect peace.*

"I'm Worn Out"

MARGARET'S STORY

"I've already driven ten miles past burnout," Helen said. "I'm exhausted and don't have the energy to keep going."

The support group I'm in listened to her. I was afraid Dora would speak up and tell her what to do to get beyond burnout. She usually offers advice, but this time she only nodded.

"This group is the only thing that keeps driving me on this non-ending expressway," Helen added.

Several others spoke up to console Helen and to express compassion. Eventually, the suggestions poured out on how to combat caregiver fatigue (a term I like better than burnout).

I decided to stay on familiar roads. "Don't take him into a foreign country," I said, "because I've learned that the more I stay with the familiar, the easier it is for Harold."

And I thought about what I did for Harold. The only time during the week he wanted to get dressed was on Sunday. He insisted on a suit and tie. (I had to learn to tie it for him.) He picked up his worn Bible and kept it in his hand. He's a member of the men's Bible class, and they take care of him while I go to my own class. Those 50 minutes are one of the ways I find wonderful relief for me.

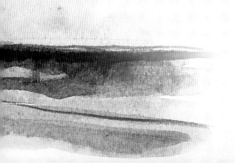

I create space for myself because it enables me to take care of him. I don't want to drive ten miles past burnout.

21

Learning to Pray Again

CONNIE'S STORY

For a few months my prayers were the quick-emergency kind. I was in too much turmoil to stop and pray. But something happened recently.

One morning I sat beside the bed and decided to pray until my husband awakened. I must have prayed at least 20 minutes, and mostly I begged for a miracle. He was the subject of most of my fervent prayer—and my prayer to enable me to cope with his increasing dementia.

About six months ago, my prayer time became significant. Vital. As important to me as eating. I grabbed on to this almost by accident. One night I was almost finished praying and I said, "Teach me, Lord, what I need to learn from this experience."

I didn't hear God speak. I didn't have a miracle. But these words came into my mind so strongly: *Do you really want to learn?*

As I pondered those six, simple words, I wasn't sure, and yet it seemed to be right. "Yes," I said aloud. "Yes, teach me."

I didn't like the lessons I learned over the next month. I saw my selfishness, my lack of patience, my agitation when my husband didn't respond. "Am I really like that?" I asked, and I didn't need to hear a voice again. I knew I was.

"Forgive me," I whispered in the darkness of the bedroom. "Teach me to serve my husband as fully as if I served you."

God gave me my miracle: I felt peace and it has stayed with me.

"The peace I give is a gift the world cannot give. So don't be troubled or afraid" (JOHN 14:27).
Lord, you said those words.
Remind me that they are for me.

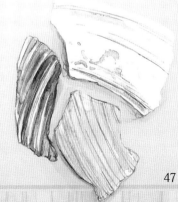

Praying Time

DAVID'S STORY

Emma's parents took her to church when she was 10 days old. When she was 71, she figured out that she had missed Sunday church only 12 times during her life. (Four of them were during the birth of our children, one time she had surgery, and the others were because one of our children was sick and she stayed home with them.)

That's the past. Emma hasn't been inside a church in three years. Our church now has a new pastor, and his style of worship is different. Emma moved around and sometimes made distracting noises and disturbed others.

Now we have our church at home. I don't like that, but it's the best we can do. Each Sunday morning we watch two different church services on TV. Both programs print the words of hymns at the bottom of the screen so we can sing with the congregation. I don't know if she can read the words, but when they sing a familiar hymn, she joins with them.

At the end of the second program, I turn off the TV, take her hands, and I pray. She doesn't often respond, but one time she leaned over and kissed my cheek. How much she grasps isn't of concern to me. I'm grateful to God for my wife of 51 years. Despite her dementia, this is special to us. We met in church, and most of our friends were members. We don't see those friends much these days, but Jesus Christ is still with us.

So we pray. And I thank God that we're still together. She is already leaving me with her dementia, and one day her body will leave.

Thank you, Lord, that you love us, are with us,
and her hands in mine remind me that we're still together.

Making the Minutes Count

Part of my life is slipping away. He's been my life for nearly 50 years. As I watch his slow descent, I feel as if he takes part of me with him.

At first (and for weeks) I felt depressed, as if I were dying right along with him. I called on my old friends at church, and I asked them for prayer. A few prayed for me on the phone. Four people came to the house to visit.

Those friends helped me see life differently. Over a period of two weeks, I decided that I couldn't change his condition. I could watch, care, and pray for him. I also decided something else: I wanted this time together to count—to mean something *to me*.

My life isn't over and neither is his. No sudden massive coronary took him, but a slow, insidious disease that regularly steals a small piece of his brain.

I wanted to make this a special time for him—as much as he could understand. I took him to McDonald's one day for an Egg McMuffin. Another time we stopped for ice cream. I had to help him with the cone, but the pleasure on his face was worth the effort.

I bring out picture albums. He doesn't recognize his parents or his siblings, but he still recognizes the little boy he was once.

We used to dance, and although he was never very good, he enjoyed it. I bought a few CDs from the big-band era, and we dance for a few minutes. He stands and moves a foot as if he still wants to dance, but that's about all. And it's enough: He understands.

Sometimes it's difficult to think of new things to do, and then I remind myself I don't have to do new things. I want him to enjoy the old as long as he can.

24

Learning About Me

"I never thought I could find the personal blessings in caregiving," she said. "I constantly thought about Ralph and sadly watched him decline. One day I realized that I can't change circumstances, but I can learn about myself."

She focused on her moods, thoughts, and desires. She spent more time with her own thoughts as Ralph's disease progressed, and she began to "dig deeper into myself." She said she had never been an introspective person, but being confined at home pushed her to look more seriously at her life.

"I wanted my life to have meaning," she said, "and I've found it. These aren't the circumstances I would have chosen, but I continue to grow spiritually as I serve my husband and remind myself that this is also service to Jesus Christ."

I can't change circumstances,
but I can change myself.

Appendix

TAKE CARE OF YOURSELF

1. Ask for help. You—the caregiver—are at an increased risk for depression and illness, especially if you don't receive support from family, friends, your church, and the community.

2. Continue to ask for help. Your loved one will change, and your burdens will become more demanding.

3. The person you love isn't who he or she used to be. The behavior can become increasingly difficult. Remind yourself, "This is the way it is."

4. At the end of each day, say two things aloud to yourself:

   • "Today I did the best I was capable of doing." That doesn't mean you were perfect, but you did what you could.

   • "All I can do is all I can do." Repeat the words until they calm you and help you realize that you can't do everything you want. You do only what you can.

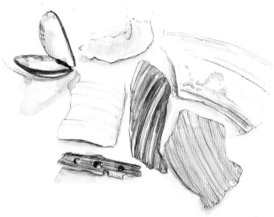

5. Go online. Read books and magazines. Learn everything you can about Alzheimer's disease and dementia.

6. Join an Alzheimer's mutual-help group (or start one). Associate with others who have similar situations. Share resources and information.

7. Consider using adult day care or respite services to ease the day-to-day demands of caregiving. Such services allow you to have a break and still know your loved one is cared for.

8. Think about the future—your future. Investigate long-term care facilities. Talk to Medicare, Medicaid, or your insurance provider to learn what help you can expect.

COMMUNICATING WITH
YOUR LOVED ONE

1. Use simple words and short sentences. Speak in a calm voice.

2. Don't treat your loved one as if he isn't present. Speak directly to him as much as possible. Insist that visitors do the same.

3. Don't try to talk above other noise such as the TV. When she talks, turn the volume to mute or turn off the set.

4. Make eye contact. Call the loved one by name. Don't speak unless you have his attention. Insist that visitors do the same.

5. Allow her to respond after you speak. Relax. Don't interrupt. If she searches for a word, gently suggest what you think she means.

6. Keep your language upbeat and positive. Even if he doesn't understand the question, your voice can enable him to relax.

7. If you can't understand what she means, and her agitation or words sound serious, say gently, "I don't understand. Please help me." Then listen.

EXERCISE AND ACTIVITIES

1. Allow him as much independence as possible. Let him do what he can while he can.

2. Set up a daily exercise time *for yourself*. Don't tell yourself, "I get enough exercise taking care of her." You need stress-relieving movements such as a walk or a few minutes on a treadmill.

3. Remind yourself that exercise usually helps her sleep better. And it can do the same for you.

4. Encourage him to move. Hold his arm and gently encourage him to stand. Take a few steps with your hand on his arm. The more active he is, the easier he'll be to manage and the better he'll feel. *And the better you will feel.*

5. Be realistic in your expectations of what she can do in exercise. Start slowly and build up duration and intensity as much as she is able. Perhaps walk together 100 feet the first day and increase it as you see how well she handles it.

6. Watch for signs of exertion or discomfort.

7. Ask about exercise programs in your area. Some senior centers have group programs. Walk inside a local mall, especially when the weather is bad.

EXPECTING THE UNEXPECTED

1. As the disease progresses, he may become incontinent. (Discuss the problem with your doctor.) Remind yourself that this happens because of the illness.

2. Accidents will occur. Stay calm. If you remain calm over a broken dish, you encourage her to do the same. Your voice often sets the tone for her response, even if she doesn't understand what happened.

3. Be prepared for uncharacteristic behavior such as "sundowning," when he may become irritated or restless in the late afternoon. Remind yourself that it's a natural (although unexplainable) phenomenon and not a conscious form of behavior.

4. She may experience hallucinations and see, hear, smell, taste, or feel something not there. She may have delusions. She may develop false beliefs and consider them real, such as accusing you of stealing her money.

5. Wandering can be a problem, especially when he gets out of the house in the middle of the night. Do whatever you can to prevent his getting outside. If he does wander, don't blame him or yell

at him. Make sure he wears some kind of identification such as a bracelet. Notify your neighbors that he tends to wander.

6. Don't let her drive. Calmly lead her to the passenger's side. If she objects, smile and say softly, "I thought I'd drive today" or "It's my turn to drive."

7. Holidays can be hectic. For some, happy memories of the past contrast with the difficulties of the present. Be sensitive to your loved one's depression or sadness.

HELP YOUR VISITORS

1. Encourage visitors, even if he doesn't remember who they are. Human connection has value.

2. Plan to have visitors at the time of day when she is normally at her best. And if it turns out to be a bad day, call and reschedule the visit.

3. Encourage your visitors to remain calm and quiet and to avoid using a loud tone of voice. Ask them not to treat him as if he were a child.

4. Ask them to call her by name, make eye contact, and not to speak unless they have her attention.

5. Ask them to respect his personal space and not to get too close.

6. Tell them to use her name frequently when addressing her.

7. Tell your visitors, "Please remind him who you are. He may not recognize you, but do it anyway."

8. Tell them not to argue if she's confused or wrong. Ask them to smile and act normal.